To Ship.
One of my
Pawsitive! FAVOR-
persa

MW00897305

Sit, Down, Stay:
Dog Training so Easy
a Human can do it

Love Dozer

Sit, Down, Stay: Dog Training so Easy a Human can do it

Dozer P. Kingsbury

Translated by
Beverly Kingsbury

To order additional copies of this book, contact:
Xlibris Corporation
1-888-795-4274
www.Xlibris.com
Orders@Xlibris.com
41920

Contents

Acknowledgments

I would like to thank Bev's friends Erika Williams and Susan Atkins, who gave advice and editing information, which was critical for getting my message across. I also understand your friendship is very important to Beverly, and since she is important to me, I thank you again.

Scale Your Listening: *It all sounds like BLAH-BLAH to me, Dozer*

Blah, blah, blah. Are you talking to me?

I am Dozer, Beverly's beautiful Sum-ma mix, but I could be your dog. We canines are social and similar, and I'm going to help you learn how to train us (and be trained by us).

First, you are either talking to me or about me—because it's all about me. Some of your choices include lure and reward, gentle guiding, capturing, shaping, conditioning, desensitization. WHAT? Don't worry, you don't have to know what all that means; I'll guide you through the maze.

How should you train us noble wonderful creatures known as canine companions? Use treats, don't use treats, feed us raw food only, feed us only dry kibble, crate us, and don't crate us. Ugh, conflicting information is propagating faster than squirrels darting across the backyard.

There seems to be confusion about the best way for you humans to train us canines. There are hundreds of different methods, trainers, books, and instructors, and no single approach has emerged as THE approach. Some approaches are more glamorized, Hollywood hyped, and marketed better than others market; but I'm not sure popularity means accuracy.

The *Dog Whisperer* Cesar Millan, Dr. Ian Dunbar, APDT (Association of Pet Dog Trainers), and at least twenty other top trainers and organizations have different philosophies on how to work with us dogs. (And, really, I'm not that hard!) At the end of 2006, there was an article in the *San Francisco Chronicle* discussing the "training controversy" between two different philosophies. In that same year, the U.S. Humane Society sent a letter of reproach regarding one of Hollywood's best-known trainers. Therefore, if the top dogs are arguing, the rest of us in the pack are bound to be confused.

The problem can be quite exasperating when you people seek knowledge, particularly when the information in some books directly contradicts material found in other books or DVDs.

If you have visited the dog section of any bookstore or pet store or library, you have probably been overwhelmed with what to read or watch; there are so many materials available. If you attempted to learn from more than one source, you could end up very confused: one book said not to play tug-of-war, a different book said play it, it's good for the dog. What do you believe? What do you do? Beverly and I see many dog owners paralyzed from information overload, and that's even before they turn to the tons of data on the Internet.

We also have pet boutiques, pet bakeries, pet sitters, doggie day care, dog hotels, dog psychics, dog walkers, and an ever-increasing industry surrounding pets. In addition, everyone has an opinion on what is best for "your" dog. (I put quotes around *your* because everyone knows we dogs own the humans.) None of the opinions are the same, but the humans are adamant about their beliefs, so bewilderment grows.

Of course, into this mix of methodologies, we can also throw in the folks who don't think they need to do anything different than their folks did in raising us fantastic hounds. They think no information is needed; problems can be solved or ignored as they arise. Animal shelters are filled with many returned dogs raised under this methodology.

Humans are not the only ones suffering from all the confusion. Look around: fearful shaking dogs, lunging dogs, dogs running away from owners into streets and being killed, dogs biting humans, dogs tearing at other dogs, animal shelter and rescue organizations filled to the max, and all that incessant barking. It could drive you crazy!

I know why there is so much confusion. We have been listening to humans trying to explain how canines behave. It is time we started listening to dogs. This is why I feel compelled to relate what I know. Let's clear up this uncertainty now.

I have a unique understanding of the situation; I have spent a lifetime intimately involved with the communication between dogs and humans, and my perspective is very simple yet relevant. We need to help resolve the mystification so humans can stop yelling, and dogs can feel safer (or as humans want to state—everybody can be happier).

The human I live with calls it Balance. She began to notice that some dogs would learn a word or command, but rarely listened to their human. The puzzle was why some of us dogs listen and others do not. Alternatively, why would one dog listen to one human, but not another human? Then she noticed that sometimes, when I got out of Balance, I even had a hard time listening as well; and she really thinks I'm well behaved, so for her, it was a puzzle.

What makes us want to listen? That is why you need to understand how Balance is the magic to good behavior. In a way, giving us dogs Balance is giving us love, and that is something we can appreciate.

I've decided to assist Bev; she studies and reads and takes classes, yet she really needs my leadership on this one. I want to help her solve this puzzle.

Let me formally introduce myself. My name is Dozer P. Kingsbury; I was named after my behavior when I wanted to get to my mother's milk bar. There was only room for eight, and I was the ninth puppy. So I simply put my head down, plowed into several of my siblings, and flipped them out of the way so I could get something to drink. Apparently this reminded some children that were watching me of a bulldozer; hence my name Dozer. The P. doesn't stand for anything. It just sounds classy, don't you think?

People have mistaken my name to mean I sleep a lot—but that is just because I'm secure, safe, and relaxed. I have BALANCE. For example, I happened to sleep most of the time the humans were taping a television show about canine good citizens. I came along to demonstrate. I demonstrated, then relaxed, and slept while the humans chatted. I was in BALANCE; I was not named Dozer because I sleep a lot! Good grief! Humans!

Anyway, I am a little over three human years old—fully an adult in dog years—and a handsome canine to be sure. My lineage is very muddled. I'm not even sure my littermates all had the same father. My mother lived with a homeless person and found a variety of places to sleep. When people ask what breed am I, my human calls me a "Sum-ma." Sum-ma this and sum-ma that. Probably some Chow, Akita, German Shepherd, Rottweiler; and who knows, I guess—just dog. I weigh a trim sixty-three pounds, with a beautiful soft rusty golden coat, noble head, and regal bearing.

I know that breed stuff is important to some humans, but we dogs don't care one lick. Amazingly, the first thing humans ask each other about the dogs on their leash is "what is it?" With a quick sniff, I can tell more about a dog than ten pages of breed and temperament pages, and I can detect the dog's daily activities for the last several days. My main concern is if that dog is safe for me to be around and where we are in a pecking order. I don't care who his parents were, or what his breed is supposed to be like. His smell tells me almost everything I need to know. Then I watch him. I watch his ears, tail, stance, eyes, face, mouth, body position. That information is worth an afternoon of yakking by humans. (We will cover this communication business in more detail in another section of this book.)

Enough of how silly humans are trying to understand me; let me bark the truth.

Since my human—Bev—seems to communicate well with both me and other humans, I will let her tell my story, so I hope her editing is accurate. Bev has a list of books at the end of this book that she has read and has helped her translate my important information.

Let's see where to begin. I suppose it might be helpful to start at the beginning. The beginning for me is not the training manual that talks about commands; it's getting me ready to be able to listen to humans. It's showing me love by giving me what I need. Since I feel safe, happy, and content and can listen to what you humans want when I'm in BALANCE, let's talk about how to give me Balance. It's just five easy steps.

Balance by Using the S.C.A.L.E. © Method of Listening

S Is for Socialization

Since there seems to be such confusion about how to train my fellow species, I want to make this very simple. I would love you to remember the five basics for helping your canine be and stay in BALANCE. I have seen those balance scales in the antique stores. I think it may help you humans remember how to BALANCE your pet.

Use a S.C.A.L.E. © for Balancing us canines.

S. Socialization
C. Communication
A. Affection
L. Leadership
E. Exercise

So keep that S.C.A.L.E. in mind as we continue our journey through the maze of dog training.

I loved being a young pup. Everything was so much FUN. I loved exploring everything. When I was with my littermates and Mom, almost nothing scared me. I looked to Mom; if she was not afraid, then why should I be; so I got great direction. When I was separated from my very first family or pack, it was scary. I was introduced to my current guardian after a very bad bout with another human. Lots of stuff scared me by then. It took me several weeks to realize this human (Bev) was going to provide me a real home, and I was somewhat safe here. I began to think of her and her darn cat as my pack. (Later another littermate, who was scheduled to be euthanized at a shelter for aggressive, antisocial behavior, became part of our pack as well. However, that did not occur for another year.)

Humans do not sound right, they look funny, and they certainly do not smell like dogs. But my new human's voice made me feel pretty good; and she was calm, gentle, yet gave me lots of rules, (we will talk more about this in the *L* section) sort of like my real (canine) mom. Bev also gave me food and played with me, and soon I understood this human was mine. So one of the first important things on the scale for balancing us dogs (me particularly) began. The *S* is for "socialization."

Socialization is the process where we are introduced to everything we might end up encountering in life. We need many repeated positive exposures to all sorts of people, other dog, other animals, places, and things.

That simply means letting me happily be introduced to everything I may encounter as I grow up. "Happily" means humans need to help me feel safe. They have to use that voice that tells me there is nothing to it. Do not use that soothing "it's OK" voice that scares the poop out of me. Also if you start to pick me up or touch me if I'm a bit timid upon meeting something new, you really make me believe there is a problem. Just use a calm, matter-of-fact voice; let me explore and use those yummy special treats so I can have a wonderful association between the treat and the new exposure.

Let me meet EVERYTHING. When we are young (about three to four months old), we probably need to meet one hundred new dogs a month as well as one hundred new people. They need to be all types of dogs and people, and all kinds of animals. Big ones, little ones, all breeds (dogs), old people, tall people, men with hats and beards, people of various sizes and ethnicity, as well as cats, birds, squirrels, turtles, and rabbits. Meeting means I am on the floor, not in your arms. It means people pick me up and touch me all over. I do mean ALL over. This made it much easier for the vet and groomer to touch me because I was so use to it. Please do not leave me alone with little people; children are often a bit rough with me, but make sure we have plenty of supervised time together.

Make sure I meet other household pets in a calm, gentle way. I must tell you, I chase cats. I cannot help it; they trigger something in me. However, the way I was introduced to my pack's cat Itty-Bit Rusty means I do not chase that cat in the house. In fact, I even sleep in the same bed with him. I cannot believe I said that. So how did that happen?

If I remember correctly, the human would not let me see or touch the cat in the beginning, but she got his smell all over me, and my smell all over the cat. She would take a slightly damp washcloth and rub it all over me to get my smell, and then run it all over the cat. She did the same to me with the cat smell. She must have let the cat in the family room when I was not there because I could smell him all over the place. After a few days, I was taken out to the deck and looked through the glass door and saw my human gently stroking that darn cat. After several more days, I could see and smell the cat through the screen door as Bev stroked him. Then one day, after a very long run when I was exhausted and sleeping calmly, my human quietly brought the cat in—carried in her arms—sat down near my bed, and stroked the cat while I was told to sit and stay. We did that for a few days, when one day, she let me go over to the cat and sniff while the cat was above my head on my human's lap. Immediately after my sniff, I was told to lie down and given some steak. Soon, I just sort of accepted that darn cat. Even after almost three years, I still try to block the cat from getting to the human, but he manages to either walk right under me, or jump over me to her lap. That stupid cat has never learned the rules, but I continue to try to teach him. Therefore, we live in a peaceable truce. We are never left alone unsupervised for more than a few minutes. I wonder if my human does not quite trust me. OK, I do chase him outside, and I go a bit bonkers when I see stray cats wondering around outside, but shhhheeeeh, I get it, no chasing Itty-Bit inside. Anyway, if I can become social with a CAT, you can probably socialize the dog in your life to anything.

Do not think socialization means introducing us to just people or animals; it also means habits. Habits such as crate training, brushing, nail trimming, bathing, ear cleaning, tooth brushing, and having our bodies touched, restrained, or manipulated. We need to accept all your customs, habits, and how life will treat us, particularly when we are young and reinforced as we age. We do not generalize very well, so being comfortable with women does not mean we feel good around men. Therefore, the most varied introductions you can provide are best.

Habits mean routine, and I love routine. It gives me comfort and tricks the humans into thinking I am well trained. Once, a human friend came to our home, and my brother and sister and I (remember we all weigh about sixty to seventy-five pounds) went charging to the door, and my brother Bizy's owner tried to open the door. We barked so vehemently, the person at the door went away, almost in tears! Soon Bev made us practice a very different habit. First, I would practice by myself with Bev, and then my sister would join us and eventually my brother. Bev would ring the doorbell, tell us to go downstairs (a word we learned and then we practiced separately), and then stay (another word we practiced for months). Now when I run downstairs away from the front door after the doorbell rings, stop barking after two barks, sit, and wait for my human to say "come," everyone thinks I am so well behaved. Silly humans! My actions just became a habit, and now some humans think Bev trained me well!

Anyway, back to habits. I love having my teeth brushed, because I know we do it every day just before we put my leash on for a walk. As a puppy, my human started all these habits as fun games. For teeth brushing, she started with yummy dog toothpaste on my baby teeth, and she just let me chew the toothbrush like a toy in the beginning. She also used that tone that said this was going to be fun. Slowly, she actually began brushing one or two teeth at a time. Now she can actually hold my muzzle and brush one-fourth of my mouth at a time. She always uses that fun voice, and I know we do it and then we go for a walk. She also feels calm so there is no reason for me to worry.

Another habit we developed: I run into the shower when I hear "bath time" because I know I get a great milk bone after the torture—I mean bath—is over. In addition, my human gives me many massages during the bath time, and a fun voice, so it is not so bad. I cannot remember when we started this routine; I just know bath time means milk-bone time. I guess we started by just walking into the shower, walking out, and getting a treat. We gradually got used to the water and door closing and the soap, so it was no big deal. Especially because Mom feels calm, using the happy voice, and never smelled or sounded as if she was afraid, AND there are treats!

How do these habits begin? Routines help. Doing the same things repeatedly until I know exactly what to do. For example, every time a bike comes near us, I sit to the left of my human and wait until it passes, then we continue. I learned this by doing it, being given a treat for it, then repeating the habit again and again. After a while, the treats stopped, but I wanted to do the routine; it gives me comfort to do something I know so well.

Therefore, good training means just great habits. It also means meeting everything: vacuum cleaners, bikes, skateboards, buses, wheelchairs, umbrellas, sprinklers, elevators, loud noises, and everything you can think of. If I am a bit fearful, just use that matter-of-fact voice and pair the sight of the new item with the most delicious treats. I never get steak pieces unless Bev is introducing me to something new, and I start out not liking it. I remember that recently I started to chase a skateboarder. Therefore, Bev and I went to a skateboard park. She sat me some distance away, talked confidently, telling me that they were just old skateboards. I was told to sit, and then the best part came; she fed me steak pieces. Then we sat closer and closer to the park, and I still got these great steak pieces. After a while, instead of feeling like lunging after those wheelie things, I felt like I wanted some STEAK. Who cares about the skateboarders! After a few weeks, we sat right next to the fence with those crazy kids whizzing by me, and every time I just sat there, I got steak! Soon there was nothing to it; skateboards were a habit, and I got very use to them.

Something humans do not seem to get: if I do not use something, I lose it. Habits are only good as long as you keep doing them. My human and I do not usually get around many children, especially now. When I was with my littermates, I sort of remember loving the wee human ones around me, but that was a long time ago. Recently, one small one would come close to Bev and I, and I became uncomfortable. Therefore, we went to this place called a kids' park, and even though I used to feel very good around kids, I forgot how. So I was fed steak and sat closer and closer to the park until I almost liked having the kids come over and feed me steak. Now Bev makes an effort to bring me around children on a regular basis. I think I like kids now even more than she does.

More memories about habits and training. I remember when I was about ten months old, my brother Bizy and I were given what Bev called a test. She wanted to see how well we had been socialized. So we went to downtown San Francisco to Union Square during the Christmas rush. There were buses and cable cars, funny costumed Santas ringing bells and billions of people walking very close together. Occasionally a dog would walk down this maze of people on a leash, and sometimes I could smell some animals in those very tall buildings. There were many noises—many of them new—a lot more people at one time than I ever remember seeing, and many very strange odors. However, my mom was calm and walked at a great fast pace, asked us to stop at every curb—just as we practiced back home. She said "heel" and "forward," and we remembered to sit when she stopped. Bizy and I felt comfortable because we were doing our commands that were familiar habits. Our human was very proud of us. People were commenting on what big well-behaved dogs we were. I began to strut and smile. Then it happened.

We passed a store with a fifteen-foot bronze statue out in front of the store. Bizy and I had never seen a statue or anything made of bronze or a fifteen-foot thing like this before. I was scared to death. I began barking and lunging and telling this thing to back off and do not tangle with my brother and me! Bizy took my cue and began to frantically bark as well. People began to point at us and laugh at what big dogs we were and how afraid we were of a statue. My human was cool. She went over in her matter-of-fact voice and said, "You silly geese, this is just an old statue." Then she hugged it. How many humans hug statues in downtown San Francisco? This calmed me a bit, but what really helped was we were told to "sit" (a habit I felt comfortable with), and Bev gave us steak. I gave a few more barks, just to let that thing know who was boss. Bev again stepped between the statue and me (which is what dog leaders do, but we will discuss that later), told me quiet and sit, and gave me some more steak. Later that day, we walked in the park and had to pass about twenty-five bronze statues, and after about the fifteenth one, they were not so scary anymore. Especially, since Bev was giving out steak after we passed one without barking.

So do you get what I mean? We need you to introduce us dogs to as many different people, dogs, and things as possible in a fun, game-type way. Remember, use a happy voice with a very calm demeanor. Also, use previous habits or commands I already know very well and treats to help me over timid spots. Please do not say "it's OK, it's OK" in a soothing voice. That makes me more scared. In addition, if you touch me or pick me up, you sort of tell me that you want me to be afraid. I am unintentionally reinforced (picked up or held or touched) when I act fearful. Please be aware of what you are teaching me. Socialization should begin early and continue throughout our lives.

Bizy remembers when he was just nine weeks old how he loved walking on the sidewalk to a local neighborhood coffeehouse; lots of different people loved him up, and he occasionally met with strange dogs. Now, anyone—or any dog—does not faze him. I wish I knew Bev during that time; I did not meet her until I was five months old. Now, I help give puppies what Bizy used to get as a pup. I am part of the socialization time in Bev's puppy classes. The puppies learn to both play with each other and respectfully ask to play with me. Therefore, to help socialize your new young pup, you should enroll it in a good kindergarten puppy class. How can you tell a good one? Well, all the students should be under six months old. The floor should be free of dog elimination—which means enzyme cleaner and poop bags nearby—the area should be fenced so there is time for safe off leash, supervised play. There should be a limited number of pups preferable similar in size with a good caring teacher. In addition, of course, they should on occasion bring in a masterful older dog to share his wisdom with the young ones.

These classes should have plenty of play and socialization time. A good class will also have games that encourage socialization like Pass the Puppy (so all pups are handled by strangers in the class), meet a big old dog (like me), be introduced to weird stuff—like the teacher wearing a motorcycle helmet while using a walker. The pups should be curious and later learn how to sit while this strange stuff passes by. All this makes a great puppy class. The commands that are introduced are not that important, and they are almost all similar from teacher to teacher anyway.

Socialization can make the difference between me being a confident, happy dog, and a dog that goes through life scared of everything. For example, in one of our puppy classes, we had a tiny Rat Terrier named Cookie—about three pounds—who came to class being held by her human mom. When the time came for all the pups to play, Cookie's mom did not want to put Cookie down. In that same class, there were young lab pups and pit bull pups that were three to five times the size of Cookie. Cookie and her mom were terrified.

The rules of puppy play are:

1. No humans touching their own dog during playtime. We young dogs need to learn to play with the other dogs and not rely on our familiar play with our humans.
2. If you have a shy dog, humans can stand near the wall—about two feet away—and let that be a safe zone for your shy pup. In other words, if your pup goes behind you for safety, you don't pick him up or talk to him; but you do gently push other pups away, so the dog who loves you can find isolation behind his human.
3. About every minute, you go over and grab your pup's collar, stop his play, say gotcha, give him a treat, and let him return to play. Later, this will build to an emergency sit (the ability for pups to listen and obey the sit command, even in the middle of dog-to-dog play). This can be very difficult, unless we practice all the time and build up to this difficult feat.

During the first week, Cookie stayed behind her human, and her mom looked as if she was angry and would not come back to class.

Gratefully, Cookie's mom did return; and during the second week, Cookie sort of became interested in the pup play, but stayed pretty much behind her mom. By the third week, Cookie was taking down the Lab and Pit during some great playtime. Now that rat terrier has a chance to become a content, happy, playful dog, not one that shakes with fear and terrified in her mom's arms. Later, when she met me, she did just fine!

This does bring up a big controversy between veterinarians and behaviorists. I am at my peak social learning time between the ages of about three and twelve weeks. But the vet often says, "Keep the dog inside, isolated until all their shots have been given." That would make me almost four months old! Cheeezze, I am almost into the fear imprint stage. Now instead of stuff being fun, I could be more afraid. So here is what I think. Use some common sense. After the second out of the set of three combination shots, start to take us out into the public. Try to stay away from where there is dog elimination. Stay on the sidewalk, not the grass or sand where filth can hide more readily. Before you let us young canine pups meet strange dogs—on leash—ask the owner if their pet is fully vaccinated. If they are, great, let us sniff each other and say hello. The last shot is often the rabies shot. So do not walk in the woods or let us young pups out at night when we could meet rabid wild animals.

Experience and statistical data support the relative safety and lack of transmission of disease in puppy socialization classes over the past ten to twelve years in the United States. In fact, the risk of one of us young canines dying because of infection with distemper or parvocirus is far less than the much higher risk of us dying (euthanasia) because of a behavioral problem. Many veterinarians are now suggesting new puppy socialization classes because they recognize how critical socialization and training is for young pups.

If you are told total isolation for your pup, discuss with your vet that you have common sense and would like to start the learning process. See what that old vet says.

Remember, socialization is not just for puppies, we old hounds will lose what we do not use, so continue to bring us around lots of new stuff. Do not keep us cooped up in the backyard, please. Those poor junkyard dogs (dogs that stay cooped up in the house and backyard only) can't go anywhere because they probably bark and overreact to everything. They are not well socialized, or they lost it. Now they are too difficult to take anywhere, so it is easier just to leave them home, and they are forced to continue staying in their large prison cells. The longer they stay isolated, the less comfortable they become around anything new, and the more likely the humans will keep the dogs in the nonthreatening backyard. It is a huge vicious cycle. Then, the more bored these junkyard dogs become, the more they will dig, bark, not listen to humans, and run around like mad dogs. That makes it more difficult to take them anywhere. You see where this is going—a dog that is not happy or balanced and acts up, producing the human who is not fully enjoying living with the four-legged pack member, and the situation only gets worse. Bottom line, we need constant socialization; after all, we are pack animals!

Balance by Using the S.C.A.L.E. © Method of Listening

C Is for Communication

Use a S.C.A.L.E. © for Balancing the canines.

S. Socialization
C. Communication
A. Affection
L. Leadership
E. Exercise

Blah, blah, blah, blah, blah, blah, blah, blah. That is what your language sounds like to me. You make sounds that are incomprehensible to our great species. You use those fingers to point, and your body posture does not tell me a thing. We are very confused by your communication, yet you expect us to learn, while you stay totally ignorant of our communication. Just imagine what that must feel like. Suppose you were beamed up to Mars, where the verbal communication was all clicks and beeps, made by creatures that looked like TV screens with snakes coming out the sides. You were tossed into a vat of Jell-O, and you had to guess what they want next. Now you are beginning to get a sense of what we go through trying to figure out what you want.

Therefore, to get balance, we canines need two aspects of communication. First, we need to clearly understand what you are saying; and second, we need you to understand what we are saying.

Let's start with your communication to us.

Here are a few simple rules:

1. Please use the exact same sounds each time you mean the same thing. For example, if you say "come" to mean "recall," please do not say "Come here," "Come over here," and "Come to me, over here, come, come, come." All those reverberations sound like different words to me. It even makes it easier if you use the same tone and inflection each time you say the exact same word. Remember, we can easily mix up your words. For example, Bizy often mistakes the word "easy" (take the treat gently) for his name Bizy. A dog named Kit can easily hear "sit" instead of his name. I guess that means be careful of the words you ask us to learn. They should be unique enough to avoid confusion.

2. Please say my name, or use a voice that lets me know you are talking to me. I usually ignore most of your vocalizations, unless I know you are talking to me. Help me know you are talking to me.

3. I listen to your intonation more that your words. I need to know you mean business. A high, soft voice does not tell me you are serious. A high-pitched voice sounds like my littermates fooling around—sounds that I can easily ignore. A lower growl from my mom meant I had to pay attention. In addition, the same is true for lower voices, with a bit of a bark.

4. If you are trying to teach me a word, make sure you are very consistent. If you say "come" and I run off and chase a squirrel, how do I know you mean "recall"? If I run off and chase a squirrel every other time you yell "come", how do I know that word doesn't mean "recall" when I'm not running after a squirrel? If you yell "come" and I do not move, and you come and get me, how do I know that word doesn't mean "stay there, I will come get you"? If sometimes I chase squirrels, sometimes I do not move and sometimes I return to you, how do I know what "come" means? Inconsistency means I really have no concept of what a word might mean, and I could guess to try to please you. If, on the other hand, every single time you said "come", I had a leash attached

and came running back (or gently pulled back) and ended up sitting in front of you, I would have no doubt what that word meant. After months of practice, this word would become a habit. Then the leash could be unattached, and I would respond correctly.

5. You need to stay calm. When you get angry, frustrated, or upset, I do not understand; and it upsets me. This interferes with my learning. This does not make learning fun. I BALK.

6. I love to learn both hand signals and verbal cues.

7. I do not like to be touched when you are trying to teach me how to do something. Gentle guiding often makes it more difficult for me to learn. For example, if you push my bottom down to teach me to sit, it takes me longer to learn what you want of me. Do I sit when you come near me, when you say the word, when you hand signal me, when you touch me; I am very confused. Sometimes I think you are playing a game where I am supposed to resist your touch! As you push my bottom down, I try to keep it up because it's fun, and I think that is what you want. So please, just lure me into position, do not physically push me.

8. I love when you teach me in very short sessions, about one to three minutes, ten times a day.

9. We canines live in the moment; please give me feedback within two seconds—I said two seconds—of my actions. Therefore, when you say "good boy," I need that within two seconds of my good behavior. The same is true of behavior that is correctable. I have to get the feedback immediately and no later than two seconds. If I soil the carpet and you walk in ten minutes later and scold me, you have taught me all the wrong things: You teach me that you are not a very good leader; after all, I have to eliminate, and if you don't want me to eliminate, YOU ARE CRAZY. You also teach me that I had better hide my defecation because you do not like to see it. You also teach me when you leave the room that something out there upsets you, so now I have increased separation anxiety. Therefore, you taught me many things, none of them intended.

10. I respond most effectively with positive rewards. Food, praise, play, and affection will get me to do almost anything. They can help me build these habits that humans often call "training." For example, in the beginning, a piece of liver was held down at Bev's left side, and I followed that treat while the word HEEL was said. After a while, I got the idea of following that treat and staying near Bev's left leg. When Bev

is constantly telling me I am heeling just right, it helps me understand when I start to goof up, and when I am doing it just right. I really want to please that woman; after all, she has that great voice and TREATS! Anyway, it's more of a habit now, but she calls it "training."

11. Just say the command once for goodness sake. If you say it several times, I begin to think the command is many words, and I ignore the first several words. Keep it simple, silly!

These are the eleven basic commandments of communicating with us.

Now, you need to understand what we are saying. There are many books written for humans on how to read and speak dog, could you at least learn a few basics? No, a wagging tail does not always mean I'm happy; whoever started that rumor was a turkey, and told only half the truth. Sometimes I wag my tail with short little wags with my tail held high, and it is a warning not to come closer.

Since you humans deemed it necessary to goof around with the noble wolf and produce over 160 breeds, everyone's communication is a little different. Curly-tailed breeds have more difficulty using their tail to relay important information and floppy-eared dogs have the same problems communicating with the ears. At least learn a few of these generalized basics:

When we are happy, our ears perk up and go forward, eyes are wide open but relaxed, mouth relaxed and slightly opened with teeth covered, often panting, body and tail relaxed. Some of us actually look as if we are smiling. Sometimes we blink.

Sometimes we can be submissive; this includes both "active" and "passive" submissive postures. When I am feeling passive submissive, I lie down on my back, belly up. This indicates a pacifying gesture that is offered to a more dominant individual (like the human guardian). It seems as though we want to have our belly rubbed in this position—and in fact, sometimes I feel safe enough to ask for a belly rub by getting into that position. Key identifying features of this behavior include ears back, exposed belly, tail tucked in, head turned away, and indirect gaze.

Active submission is a pacifying pose used when I acknowledge another dog or human is higher ranking, or to inhibit another dog's aggression. The key identifying features may be ears back, tail hangs low or wags slowly, one paw raised, eyes half closed, and my mouth nearly closed with just the tip of my tongue darting out, maybe yawning.

The playful position is when I want to solicit play. I may bow down in front, which is a combination of submissive and dominant gestures. This stance is offered to invite another (dog or human) to play or as part of a courtship behavior. An identifying feature is that my front end of my body is lowered, as if ready to leap forward. We will often exhibit excited bouncing and jumping up and down. Circling around and running forward and back is an invitation to play. My mouth is probably open and relaxed with tongue exposed, ears up or relaxed and tail up, loosely wagging. I may have excited barking or soft play growling.

Aggressive behavior can be identified as two types: defensive aggressive and territorial aggressive. In a defensive aggressive posture, I'm fearful and am giving warning signals to indicate that I do not want to be approached, but if I am, I may attack to protect myself. The key features of this pose are ears back; pupils dilated; mouth is tense, wrinkled and snarling with exposed teeth; tail is down and tense; posture is mildly crouched with the weight over my rear legs.

Now if I'm territorial aggressive, I will try to make my body as large as possible. My ears will be forward or back and close to my head. My eyes will narrow or stare challengingly, my lips will be open, drawn back to expose my teeth; I may snarl and possibly snap or growl and bark loudly. My tail will be fluffed up and straight out from my body. My body will be tense, upright, and my hackles on my neck may be up.

Depending on the breed, these signals may vary. Curly tailed dogs' tails tell a different tale than straight tails. Wrinkly faces and pushed in faces will look differently when there is anger or joy. Watch your dog, watch him at home, or in the dog park so you can learn to read your dog. We love to be understood.

Calming signals are often used to calm ourselves or another dog. When you brush me too hard, I give you calming signals to tell you to take it easy, please pay attention. Calming signals include looking away, and this includes averting the eyes to turning the head, to turning the entire body away. My eyes tell a lot. Are they wide open, calm, staring, looking away, blinking? Watch my eyes.

Yawning, licking the air, excessive scratching, raised paw are all calming signals. Watch us, learn and react appropriately, please.

I have seen dogs that are very uncomfortable with a child around. They look away, they yawn, they lick the air, and they begin to have a wide-eyed look. When they are totally ignored, they may go on to growl or snap because no one pays any attention to his or her warning or calming signals. Then they are punished or even euthanized for becoming aggressive, and they were just trying to get someone to listen. It is very sad. Please learn to listen; we can relax if we know our human guardians understand us. No one likes to be ignored.

We cannot leave the section on communication without discussing our verbalizations:

> To us, barking is far less important than other forms of communication, such as our body language or scent marking. Still, barking, growling, howling, and whining have a place in our dictionary.

> Barking is a great way to get the attention of a human or another dog. It also announces our territory and helps relieve stress. Different barks mean different things.

> A series of high-pitched barks may mean I am worried or lonesome and want attention. A single bark in my regular voice means I am curious, alert, and am trying to make contact. Quick, repetitive high-pitched barks may mean I'm feeling playful or I want to chase something. A lower repetitive bark may be my warning bark or protective sound.

> Growling is an unmistakable warning sign. We use it to tell other dogs or humans to back off. We also growl when frightened. When I combine a growl with a dominant posture, I am probably feeling aggressive. When I combine a growl with a submissive posture, I may be feeling fearful or defensive. Of course, a growl during play is just practice and usually has no meaning.

> Howling is how we canines get in touch with other dogs, even when they are miles away. A singsong howl is used to contact other dogs and means we may be curious or happy. Plaintive, mournful howls can signal distress. Sometimes I howl or bark when I'm bored, lonely, or even under exercised.

> Whining and whimpering hark back to puppyhood when these sounds got us attention. Here is how to interpret them: when we are excited or lonesome, we will whine or whimper to get your attention. These whines can sound like yawns. When I am stressed, fearful, or worried, I will often give repetitive, squeaky whines that

may be punctuated with shrill yaps. My sister Surrie whines when she is excited and wants something NOW.

We use vocalization as more of a punctuation mark in our communication. Our body language, face, tongue, eyes, tail, and eyes are far more communicative.

I think one of the difficulties in communication is that humans are primates, and we are canines. So we use our bodies very differently. You lean forward to get attention, but that implies dominance to me. Patting my head may mean affection to you, but sometimes that implies dominance to me. When you face me and yell "come," you expect me to come toward you; in dog language, if I wanted you to come to me, I would turn around and sniff the ground.

You rely on language; I am visual, and this makes interesting differences.

As you can see, the communication part of the S.C.A.L.E. is very important. It helps us understand one another.

Balance by Using the S.C.A.L.E. © Method of Listening

A Is for Affection

Use a S.C.A.L.E. © for Balancing the canines.

S. Socialization
C. Communication
A. Affection
L. Leadership
E. Exercise

I do not want to discuss whether we love, or "affection" is a word we dogs really understand. I know I have a bond with my pack, and you humans are usually thought of as part of my pack. Since the majority of humans get dogs because they want to love them, or feel loved, this is a very touchy subject. I think it's silly when humans try to love their pets like children. We are not human, and we really do not want to be loved like one. We want the affection appropriate for a dog. Loving me means helping me get what I need, not what humans need. I know one of the rewards in life for me is the affection of my guardian—the type of affection I respect.

For the humans, affection should be the easiest part of this S.C.A.L.E., but it is often the love you humans want to give, not what we dogs want to receive. For example, I do not care for hugs around the neck or pats on the head. In fact, many dogs will tolerate hugs out of respect for their humans, but rarely do they enjoy these displays. I do love my ears scratched, my belly rubbed, and my neck and under-the-chin stroked. I love those forms of affection, would tolerate the rest from my guardian, and really do not care for other forms of affection that strangers often proffer. My brother Bizy is very different; he loves strokes on the head (not taps that can feel like a threat to us canines) and medium hard strokes on the side of his body. He also loves very rigorous back scratches. Surrie, my sister, loves her chest rubbed and the base of her tail rubbed. We all love touch—just different places and different types of strokes.

Affection also means responsibility. Let us start with adequate food at reasonable time intervals. What is good nutrition? Well, the easiest, most common is dry kibble—and dry kibble only. No canned food added in; save that for treats. The dry food should be premium, life-cycle food. My favorites include the brands that list lamb, turkey, chicken, fish, or beef as their first ingredient. If you look at what you have to feed a hundred-pound dog, you will see some brands say eight cups and some say three cups. Obviously, for approximately the same nutrition, some food has much more filler than others. In addition, what goes in must come out. There is not a need for filler—it is just expensive. After the first ingredient and the filler factor, then you can care about organic or no chemicals, or whatever else is important to you. Remember to get dog food that is specific to the dog, like large breed puppy or small dog or senior. Sometimes Bev adds some vitamin C or brewer's yeast or a tablespoon of olive oil and a cooked egg into my kibble. She thinks these additives help my skin and coat stay so beautiful.

Some folks think raw food only or cook-your-own is the way to go. I only know that the premium food makers spend huge amount of time and money figuring out optimum nutrition. Most of our humans do not have the time to produce homemade balanced meals, so kibble is a good choice. It also helps keep my teeth and gums in good order. Of course, I do not have allergies, so that is something that may have to be considered for each individual dog.

It is interesting to note that since the domesticated dog has been eating kibble, we have been living much longer than our ancestor—the wolf—or when we only ate raw food.

How about treats? They can be very important, particularly in the beginning of training. I like soft little treats because sometimes I get very excited, I can choke, and those hard ones can be murder. In the beginning, we used many treats, so I got a lot of Nature's Balance. It is really a dog food—in a tube—like salami or baloney. So while I was early in my training and getting many treats, they were healthy for me. Bev would cut it up into very tiny bites; after all, I only need a taste. With small soft nutritious treats, training was fun! Moreover, it was a dog food, so my kibbles were cut down during heavy training periods so I would not gain too much weight. My other favorite treats included Bil-Jac (soft liver plus stuff), cheese, peanut butter, tiny soft salmon, hot dogs, or carrot pieces.

Weight is another important thing about affection. Sometimes humans think feeding us table scraps is showing love. Remember we are scavengers, many of us will eat anything, anytime, and most of us will eat until we explode. A few extra pounds on a dog can severely limit our quality of life. If you could control my life span and expand it from ten years to fourteen years, wouldn't you? It is imperative to keep us at our proper weight. The easiest way to check for our ideal weight is not the scale, but it is to feel our ribs. They should feel as if they are sticking out, but you cannot see them. If you feel some fat between the ribs and the skin, we are too heavy. Bev feels my ribs every night and feeds me a little less until I reach my proper weight. Apparently, most of the packaged instructions tell the humans to feed us too much. For my size, the manufacturer suggested that I am fed three and one-fourth cups of kibble a day. Bev feeds me about two cups a day, sometimes a little less if I have had many treats. So if you love us, keep us fit!

Flea and tick medication is important and needs to be applied monthly or those bites can cause great skin irritation. Flea collars do not seem to work on most of us, and flea shampoos will not protect us over time. My favorite protection is the topical monthly applications (Revolution, Advantage, Frontline, etc.); they usually work on most of us.

Affection also means proper care—appropriate vaccinations, de-worming, proper grooming, baths, nails clipped, and ticks removed. All of which I really depend on my human guardians for. I also need daily brushing of my fur, and my teeth cleaned, neither one can I do by myself. I will need a bath occasionally. Careful, not too often, it can dry out my skin. How can you tell when the dog in your family might need a bath? Feel the fur; is it sticky or oily or dirty? Smell, does your pup have an "I need a bath" smell?

Deworming us canines is also very important. Please talk with your vet about how to prevent these parasites from invading our bodies. Bev found the Columbia Animal Hospital site very informative about worms:

http://www.petshealth.com/dr_library/wormsdog.html.

Heartworms are very deadly, with few clinical symptoms. A very good write-up on heartworms can be found at the Great Lakes Border Collie Rescue site:

http://www.greatlakesbcrescue.org/HealthNTraining/Heartworm.htm.

To help share the information about vaccinations, I have asked Bev to include some excerpts from the UC Davis Web site (http://www.vmth.ucdavis. edu/vmth/clientinfo/info/genmed/vaccinproto.html) about vaccinations.

Canine Vaccination Guidelines

Canine Core Vaccines

Core vaccines are recommended for all puppies and dogs with an unknown vaccination history. The diseases involved have significant morbidity and mortality and are widely distributed, and in general, vaccination results in relatively good protection from disease. These include vaccines for canine parvovirus (CPV), canine distemper virus (CDV), canine adenovirus (CAV), and rabies.

Canine Parvovirus, Distemper Virus, and Adenovirus-2 Vaccines

For initial puppy vaccination (< 16 weeks), one dose of vaccine containing modified live virus (MLV) CPV, CDV, and CAV-2 is recommended at 6-8 weeks, 9-11 weeks, and 12-16 weeks of age. For dogs older than 16 weeks of age, one dose of vaccine containing modified live virus (MLV) CPV, CDV, and CAV-2 is recommended. After a booster at one year, revaccination is recommended every 3 years thereafter unless there are special circumstances that warrant more or less frequent revaccination. Note that recommendations for killed parvovirus vaccines and recombinant CDV vaccines are different from the above. These vaccines are not currently stocked by our pharmacy or routinely used at the VMTH. We do not recommend vaccination with CAV-1 vaccines, since vaccination with CAV-2 results in immunity to CAV-1, and the use of CAV-2 vaccines results in less frequent adverse events.

Canine Rabies Virus Vaccines

In accordance with California state law, we recommend that puppies receive a single dose of killed rabies vaccine at 16 weeks of age. Adult dogs with unknown vaccination history should also receive a single dose of killed rabies vaccine. A booster is required one year later, and thereafter, rabies vaccination should be performed every 3 years using a vaccine approved for 3-year administration.

Canine Non-Core Vaccines

Non-core vaccines are optional vaccines that should be considered in light of the exposure risk of the animal, i.e., based on geographic distribution and the lifestyle of the pet. Several of the diseases involved are often self-limiting or respond readily to treatment. Vaccines considered as non-core vaccines are canine parainfluenza virus (CPiV), distemper-measles combination vaccine, *Bordetella bronchiseptica, Leptospira spp.*, and *Borrelia burgdorferi*. Vaccination with these vaccines is generally less effective in protecting against disease than vaccination with the core vaccines.

Therefore, you and your vet can help us stay healthy. Humans should also understand a few basic symptoms for common diseases, and have not only their regular veterinarian's phone number handy, but also an emergency vet number for after-hours care. Know some of the common diseases, get a good vet handbook for parents, and take a Red Cross dog-saving class. Learn about some of the common ailments: bloat, overheating, worms, plugged anal glands, foxtail intrusion, poisoning, hip dysplasia, cancer, mange, ear and eye infections, kennel cough, giardiasis, and diabetes. I guess, bottom line, know the dog in your life well enough to observe any change. You know, we do not like to show a weakness like illness. Our basic survival drive makes us want to hide any defect like an illness, so you need to be very observant. By the time we readily show you how sick we are, it may be too late.

Since bloat can kill me, and most dogs, within about an hour, having emergency numbers preprogrammed in your phone can save a life. This is a very important precaution, especially if you love your dog.

Finally, I really thank you for neutering me. I do not understand the big human debate about this matter. I am far more affectionate to my human companions, I do not have sexual tension, I do not want to run to every female in heat, I do not quite have the same strong desire to mark every bush and prove who is boss. My smell does not provoke other males, so fewer males pick fights with me. I am far more relaxed and at ease. Therefore, contrary to the fear that many human males have, I thank you for neutering me. It was no big deal. I hardly felt a thing; I was playing that same afternoon (once the anesthetic wore off), and I really do not remember anything unpleasant, and I do not miss anything; I do not know anything else.

Time spent with me, interacting with me, really shows me your love. We can play ball, tug-of-war, brushing my fur, walking together; and I know you care for me. I really enjoy when we practice our commands together—it's a special time for just you and me, and I get a lot of positive feedback. I also love routine. I feel comfortable when you come home about the same time every day, and I guess that comfort is a form of love.

Do you recognize my affection? When I lean against you, it is often a combination of affection and dominance (I'm commanding a bit more space than usual). It can be equated to a man putting his arms around his girlfriend as they walk down the street. It is both affection and a bit of claiming of territory. When I come over to nudge you, I often want attention. When I calmly sit and lift my paw, I am asking for a bit of affection, or maybe to come and play. You all seem to know play bowing when I sort of bow in front of you as an invitation to play. Paw batting is also a form of play. All these are forms of affection. If I feel safe around you, I may want to play, and this can often be translated into the human concept of affection. Surrie loves to greet Bev with the "I love you" stretch. It is similar to a play bow, but not so ready to pounce. It's a form of love and respect.

Whenever I try to get close to my human's face to lick it, this is a form of affection and a form of respect. Bev read in a book that back in the days when canines were wild wolves, baby wolves would try to lick the mom's mouth, and she would drop some food into the pup's mouth. Some humans think that is why we lick the face. I am not sure why, I just want to get to her face. I have also learned to get close to human hands when I want to be stroked. Nose nudging can mean a desire for affection, or get out of my favorite chair. Sniffing to get your scent is also important for me to feel safe,

I am not sure if it is a form of affection, but when I feel safe, I can feel or want affection.

So bottom line, affection is displayed differently between humans and dogs. Affection also means providing for my needs, not just your desires. Affection and touch are important; it is one of the rewards I yearn for. However, the responsibility associated with affection is just as important.

Balance by Using the S.C.A.L.E. © Method of Listening

L Is for Leadership

Use a S.C.A.L.E. © for Balancing the canines.

S. Socialization
C. Communication
A. Affection
L. Leadership
E. Exercise

This leadership concept is one that sparks more human anger and raging arguments than anything else on the S.C.A.L.E. Many years ago, most of the dog trainers used the word "alpha." "You have to be the alpha dog, or your dog won't respect you." People were taught how to be dominate, how to "alpha roll" their dogs into submission. Most of this came from a small study of wolves, which was later shown to be flawed, misinterpreted, and statistically irrelevant. It is the stupidest thing I ever heard. I have never seen one dog or wolf roll another. I have seen a dog choose to roll over and show submissive behavior, but it is a decision based on many things; and it is a decision each dog makes for himself based on where we think we are in the hierarchy, or if I think that the other dog can beat me senseless.

In addition, after being domesticated since about AD 1200, things have changed a bit since we were wolves. I remember Dr. Ian Dunbar saying something like "Looking toward the wolf to discover how to raise dogs is like humans looking toward the orangutans for parenting advice." Although there are many urges and strong drives that I have to attribute to the fact that I share 304 out of 306 chromosomes with the wolf and seventy-eight out of seventy-eight genes, I agree with Dr. Dunbar. I also do not think of humans as dogs. I know they are a different species. So domination is a silly idea, but leadership or leverage is exactly what we need. You can call it rules, boundaries, or even habits, but we need this structure.

One of those deep drives within me that I cannot explain or rationalize is the need to survive. I need a leader within the pack to survive. A leader is not the strongest, but rather the smartest. One that can get us food, keep us out of danger, and make us feel safe. If I do not sense a leader within the pack, I may even reluctantly assume that responsibility. That responsibility can be very hard on me. If I am the leader, I need to prowl the house to protect it, I must guard against all strange things (people, animals, wheelie things) that may be a danger to our pack. I can never relax. Please give me the gift of NOT having to be the pack leader. I don't mind being the alarm; after all, my ears and nose can tell much faster than you humans when there is an intruder nearby, and my bark is usually more alarming. However, please do not make me the leader.

It's amazing to me to see how mixed up humans are about this entire concept. There was a woman who received a tiny toy Chihuahua puppy as a Christmas gift. She loved that animal. She held her "baby" up by her chest (up high in a place where leaders stay). She spoiled this puppy, giving it whatever she thought her pup needed, but no structure, no discipline, or leadership. So of course, the pup began to think he was the leader. When he weighed only two pounds and was only seven weeks old, it was too cute when he barked and yelped at anyone approaching his "mama." Later as he grew into his pack leader role, be would not allow anyone to approach his human. "Mama" thought that it was so cute how protective her baby was. Later, when her pup turned about two years old, he took this leadership responsibility very seriously, even though it made him a nervous wreck. One day, as "Mama" was shopping for clothes and holding her baby in his place of honor—by her chest—she reached for a blouse. Baby was very frightened about this foreign environment called a store, he was nervous and worried that his pack could get hurt, so he nipped Mama when she reached beyond where Baby could protect her. You can see this behavior in wolf packs; the leader will often nip at a pack member who may get ahead of the leader into potentially dangerous territory. After she was bitten, she took her pup into the shelter and asked that he be euthanized for turning aggressive. That poor Chihuahua did exactly what he was trained to do, then was given up to be put to death for doing exactly what he was suppose to do as a leader.

No matter what kind of obedience training you practice, no matter how much money you spend, we dogs will not listen unless we think you are the leader. If we are the leader, we will only listen when we want to, when there is nothing better to do. How many times have I heard humans say "my dog only listens sometimes" or "he used to be such a good dog, now he only listens in the house" or "his recall is only good on occasion, not consistently" or "he only sits when I have a treat in my hand." Well, DUH, if I thought I was the leader, why would I listen to you? Leaders do not follow.

When we dogs think of the human children as playmates, and not leaders, we can roughhouse too much with them, herd them by nipping at their heels, and we can ignore them. Obviously, leadership needs to be based on respect, not power. That is where many human males make a major mistake. They think if the dog fears them, that makes them the leader. Not true. We can feel someone is a bully, we can fear him or her, but it does not mean we want to listen to them, and may not whenever we can. It certainly does not help small children become respected leaders. So if the man shouts at the dog, uses choke collars, and shoves the dog around, he may be thought of as the bully, but not the leader. That means the moment we can, we will not listen. Being a leader of the pack is sort of like being a leader of humans. Bosses who are respected will get their team to work hard, listen, and try 110 percent. Bosses that you don't respect are ridiculed, and the team falls apart. Leadership is earned. Some very current thinking says humans need to build leverage with their canine companions.

Here are a few simple ideas on how humans can build their leadership roles:

1. Nothing in life is free. Make sure you remind us pooches that no pleasure comes without listening to you. Teach me to sit for dinner, lie down before doors are opened, etc. Because I am so very clever, you

should build a long routine that varies with every task. For example, sit, down, sit, shake, down, and stay—as one routine. A minimum of three different commands are needed, not just a memorized dance (so this is not a routine, but real listening to you). If it is a routine, I can believe it is my decision to do the routine, not the need to listen to you. Every delight in my life means I have to listen to you for several commands. With a family, if all the humans were there when I had to listen and follow the requests, I could learn that all humans where leaders—even young ones.

2. Humans go first through doorways and up and down stairs. Eventually you can teach me to sit and stay until I am released through EVERY door and at the foot of the stairs—this will not only reinforce humans as leaders, it helps eliminate tripping people on the stairs. Until dogs learn to stay and wait, they can be leashed and walked behind the humans through the door and on the stairs. Even on walks, part of the time I will need to heel so you can lead.

3. No dogs on the beds or furniture. (If you cannot abide by this rule, only allow us up by invitation—or command!) Close the door so I stay off the bed and limit my access to the living room and family room furniture when you are not there. This is important, or I will still think it is my throne, but must not sit on it in front of you.

4. **Do not repeat a command more than once**. If I do not respond on the first try, help me into position. Be sure you have plenty of treats for the next few months to help reward me for listening. If I do not listen, walk away and say SORRY not this time (no treat or reward). I love your attention, turning your back to me will be a definite sign of disapproval.

5. Ignore me if I nudge you for attention. Leaders give attention on their own terms, not when we dogs demand. Ignore me if we are constantly pushing toys at you. Leaders initiate play and decide when the game starts and ends. This keeps me on my paws because I never know when the fun begins. If I come over for attention, make me earn it first, then love me up.

6. Provide consequences, ignore what you do not like, avoid yelling at me for barking or jumping for instance. From my perspective, any attention is better than none. Speaking to me can often be mistaken for reinforcement.

I know I can relax and let Bev worry about being leader. She leads us on walks; she controls my food, my treats, my toys—all my pleasures in life. I do not have to worry about anything but having fun. In our home, when

Bev is gone, we have a special room that is only for us. It has no furniture; it has a doggie door to the outside. We have plenty of water and toys and our beds. The TV is on quietly and tuned to the food channel. (There are no scary animal sounds or weird scary noise, but I do get hungry.) Perfect! In the morning, we go through the same kind of command routine before we get our collars on for walks, before we get into the car to go to the dog parks, before we get any pleasure; we earn it!

When Bev arrives home, we have to sit before she will open the door, and then she bends her face down to us and says "free" before we can lick her face and welcome her home. Then she loves us up. Then we wait at the bottom of the stairs until she walks to the top, and she says "free," then we run up and join her in the family room. When it is dinnertime, I have to listen to, and obey several different commands—beg, crawl, sit, stay, come; and then I can eat. Or it might be down, sit, down, shake, stay, and free and then I run to my dinner plate.

At about ten every night (I do not have a watch, and I cannot tell time, but I have something internal that lets me know the time to leave the family room each night), we go to the bedroom. My sister and I wait for Bev. She showers and brushes her teeth and does some other human stuff. We are sitting or lying down and waiting for her by the bed. She finally crawls into bed, gives us several commands—maybe down, paw, beg, down, and then she says "UP." We jump into bed and have a great night's sleep.

I guess in the beginning I had to figure out who was the leader, and I might have wanted to prove that I was a better leader. Because leadership was not based on power, I wanted to listen to get my rewards; it was easy to have Bev build her leverage. Now I do not even think about leadership anymore; my behavior is mainly routine, just sort of a habit.

There are a few other behaviors leaders exhibit. When one of the dogs in my pack starts to play with another dog from another pack, sometimes a leader will separate them to prevent problems. If you ever watch at a dog park, you will often see leader dogs running in between two dogs that are either playing or beginning to quarrel. Therefore, humans that are the leaders of the pack frequently step in front of their dogs to help maintain peace. For example, if I start to bark at a dog across the street, Bev will step between me and the other dog, and tell me to sit and be quiet. Alternatively, if I begin to quarrel with another dog—lunge and growl—she steps in between us and walks toward me, so I have to back up (and away from that other dog). That behavior is very understandable to me, better than tugging on my leash and saying no; I would just pull against the leash and still try to get to that other dog. Bev, even though she is human, uses body language that I totally understand.

Leaders do not yell. They quietly but firmly tell me what they need. Yelling sounds like puppies, puppies are not leaders. Leaders are consistent; and I know I can rely on a leader.

BE A LEADER.

Balance by Using the S.C.A.L.E. © Method of Listening

E Is for Exercise

Use a S.C.A.L.E. © for Balancing the canines.

S. Socialization
C. Communication
A. Affection
L. Leadership
E. Exercise

Contrary to how I have heard most humans talk about exercise, I love it. In fact, we dogs have to have it. If we are underexercised, we have so much energy buildup; we cannot stand ourselves. We certainly cannot calm down, listen to our humans, or be content. I do not know if there is a chemical buildup or not, I only know I cannot stand still. Some dogs will run around uncontrollably, pace, or bark excessively, or chew destructively or self-mutilate, dig up the entire yard, or exhibit several of these symptoms—all because of the need for more physical exercise. When behaviorists attempt to fix a behavioral problem, the first correction they often make is, get that dog more exercise!

Big backyards do not equate to exercise. When my human was a little girl and they had a dog, that dog never left the backyard, and no one knew any better. Current research suggests that backyards become like large prison cells. They do not contain any new smells, stimulation, or reason to run around. Dogs—even when more than one—are left alone, usually lie around most of the time, use the area for elimination, then go back to napping. My sister and I have a large backyard—lots of places to climb and run—but we just lie around when the humans are gone (the video camera confirms this), so we are typical of what current science has studied.

A walk around the block is good for giving me new smells to examine, but does not do much for my muscles. No offense to Bev, but I have four legs, she has only two; therefore, she is so much slower than I am. It might be better if she could run for an hour, or have me run alongside a bike for an hour. I also need off-leash play—running on the beach, climbing the cliffs, running into the water, chasing imaginary animals, chasing a ball, digging in the sand, and just running like crazy. Off-leash play with other dogs is also great. I am not a real social butterfly with other dogs, I mean they are OK, but I usually do not play with them. When I am taken to a dog park, I often hang around the humans hoping for a spare treat. I usually just prowl around by myself. However, on occasion, I end up running with one of the dogs, or a couple of us canines will jump up and mouth one another or I pretend to stalk and run. So by the end of an hour at the dog park, I've used many muscles that I do not use on a walk around the block. Therefore, that dog park can be very good.

How can you judge a good dog park, one that will be safe for us four-legged loved ones? Fenced in, or far away from any cars for safety is good to look for. A park that separates little dogs from big dogs prevents accidents like the big dogs playing a little too rough with the wee ones. It may also prevent prey shift.

Prey shift is when a little dog is running, and one of us larger lads sees the little one from a distance and our brain is tricked into thinking we are looking at a rabbit—or other prey—not a dog. Even though we can be the nicest dog, if that prey drive goes into gear, we will run dead on to destroy that prey. That prey in this instance is a little dog, but we do not realize that until we may have destroyed the animal. Therefore, parks that separate smaller from larger dogs are good.

A park that does not have dog feces sitting around means that the owners show their responsibility. Those same owners should be attentive to their dogs, not just sit around talking with one another. This helps reduce dog tensions when the humans are watching their dogs closely, so potential quarrels can be stopped before they explode. So first, pick a good park, and then make sure you have the right behavior in the park.

Good park behavior for humans also means movement. You need to keep moving. If Bev stays in one place, I just stand around near her, and I can get territorial. Not all of us dogs are the same, but as a rule, humans need to keep moving, and we dogs will too. The exception to this is if you take one of my shy friends to the park. Then the human needs to stand near a fence and make a safe zone for a fearful dog to use. The safe zone is an area behind their human leader where they can hide, and the human keeps all dogs away. That way, when my shy friends feel like coming out to meet some dog, they will.

Weekends are not great times for dog parks because some dogs that never get enough exercise come on the weekends, and they sometimes are just eager for a quarrel. Therefore, we stay away from most dog parks on the weekends.

Other good exercises are our excursions to the beach. We may walk for two miles to the beach where we play fetch or run around exploring for about an hour. We even walk in the rain. I do not care what the weather is like; I just love to run outside. Some dogs develop a fear of bad weather, and that is directly a responsibility of how their humans raised them. Too bad that they have so many fears and cannot enjoy the world. In addition, we also play yard games. Occasionally, Bev will not feed me my meal in my bowl; she will take that kibble and throw it all over our backyard. Then my sister and I run around for twenty minutes trying to find every morsel of food. Now we are exercising our body and our brain.

The brain needs exercise too. Back in the days when dogs were wild—or we were wolves—we would spend five or six hours a day finding, hunting, and killing our food. That means we would sniff, stalk, run, sometimes miss and do it again, and finally bring down our dinner. Then it would take some muscles to tear apart our meal. Now, if the kibble is poured into my bowl, I can finish it in about two minutes. So now what do I do for the next 5 hours and 58 minutes, particularly if the humans leave the home, and I am alone?

Toys help, but not the toys that require a human to be there to make it any fun. Stuffed toys, ropes, and tug toys are boring when I play by myself. Even with my sister Surrie, we seldom play with our toys together. On occasion for about three minutes every few hours, we might play with a tug toy, but we usually wait for our human to play that game. We need toys that remind us of our hunting, stalking, and dog-type exercise. Bev calls these toys interactive, because we interact with these toys on our own, and they involve our brain. Here are a few ideas for enriching our environment:

1. Get a few Kong's (see below for examples) and fill them with unusual tastes (peanut butter with a few liver treats and/or steak and/or carrots and sealed with more peanut butter or cream cheese). You can also get some interactive toys that require us to think and work for our play or get squeaky toys hidden within cubes (commercially there are the hidden squirrel inside a tree type) or get bully sticks (make from bull muscle) in different shapes for chewing and are very digestible (unlike rawhide). Here are some examples of great interactive dog toys, and they come in sizes for little dogs and us bigger dogs:

Busy Buddy   *Buster Cube*   *Hide a Squirrel*

Egg Babies   *Braided bully sticks*   *Air Kong QTease Squirrel*

Hide a toys   *Intellibone*   *Kong's.Kong's of all sizes*

Leo's   *Holy Roller (stuffed)*   *Squirrel Dude*

More Kong's

2. Rotate our toys every two days, so they remain interesting. Introduce/ Start the new toys by playing with them with us, so we not only know how to play with the toy, but we have your association with them. After we are introduced to the toy, you may put it down only when you are gone.
3. Play a radio softly so your neighbors do not mind. This might help keep us company a bit when we are alone. After all, when you are in the house, there is conversation, TV or music playing, and noise. When you are gone, it is so quiet; it is a bit scary.
4. Provide dog games. Occasionally hide the toys or treats all around our area or in the yard and encourage us to "sniff" out our rewards.

Stimulating the mind as well as the body is important. If the only stimulation I get all day is when my human walks in the door, I get sooooooo excited seeing her—partly because I'm bored out of my mind—that I can't concentrate. Some dogs might jump up and down or run around as if they are crazy. Crazy from boredom. Please do not do that to us. Exercise our minds and our bodies every day!

Remember that we will not listen or demonstrate our training unless we are well balanced, and remain that way though out our life. OK, now that you know the S.C.A.L.E. and how to balance us, we are ready to learn how to become well-trained pooches.

Basic Obedience Commands

Training Recommendations

Here is a summary of some of things we have discussed:

1. Be patient. Enjoy, because we will definitely notice your emotions.
2. Plan. Set us up to succeed. If the family dog is not "getting it," the behavior probably needs to be broken down into smaller steps.
3. Be realistic. Do not expect me or the dog of your house to perform a behavior in an environment that is new to us. Start out in the house, proceed with your back to us—this is very distracting—then go into another room (check the success with a mirror at the door's edge), and then finally try it outside. Just because I understand what "sit" means in the living room, does not mean I understand it outside unless I have practiced it.
4. Be kind. Use positive methods to teach us what is expected of us. Stay positive.
5. Avoid punishment. I do not respect punishment, I can learn to distrust you, and I'm never sure why you are mad at me, or what you really want me to do.
6. Reward effectively. Pay up! Treats should be very tasty, but very small. *REMEMBER, ALL REWARDS MUST COME WITHIN TWO SECONDS OF THE SUCCESSFUL BEHAVIOR.*
7. Be generous. In the beginning, humans should reward with treats all the time. Then reward every other time, later every once in a while. It is sort of like gambling. If you have ever sat at a slot machine and put some coins in and occasionally you got a payoff, you kept putting in your coins. That is sort of, what happens with me. When Bev started to randomly give me treats but always praised me, I tried even harder wondering when that treat would come my way.
8. If your puppy forgot, or after several successful practices did not do it, go back to an easier form of the same task. End the session on a

success. If you leave after a failed attempt, we may think the rules of the game have changed.

9. Practice often. Teach us in short, frequent sessions.
10. Every command should be command, lure into the behavior, praise upon the act, reward, and then release. Later we will not need a treat to lure us; we respond very well when we begin to get rewards on a varied pattern. We always want praise and then a release command.
11. Commands should be one word, crisp, and well enunciated. Remember, English is our second language. Do not repeat the command, or the command repeated many times is what we will expect to hear.

House Training

If I remember correctly, management is the most effective tool you have. The key to successful house training is supervision. Watch us constantly. Use baby gates or a playpen to keep us in the same room you are in, or leash us to your chair or belt so we cannot ever be more than a leash length away at any time. If you do not see us, we are probably going potty. If you have to answer the phone or make dinner, put us in our crate or a playpen in the room you are in. By confining us to a small place, like an airline kennel, you will teach us to wait to be let out. We will be more reluctant to soil our crate or den, because if we do, we will be forced to sit and look at it and smell it until you return. When you do let us out, take us directly to our assigned toilet area and praise for quick results. Take us outside on an unfailingly regular schedule—every hour on the hour—and make every outing a party with cheering and cookies. Remember, this is not forever, just until we are house-trained.

One of your first duties is to identify what the dog in your life does right before he eliminates. Does the dog sniff? Circle? Pause midstep? Twitch their ear? Start a sniffing pattern, hold their ears in a certain position? Some dogs provide signals that are easy to spot, while others are more difficult. Watch carefully. I am easy. I sniff the ground trying to find just the right smell, and I look up in a thoughtful, still pose, and lift my leg and start. Surrie goes around and around in a circle, then repeats that process for three or four rounds. Just like a female to be so particular! Anyway, just as we begin to show signs, you can redirect and respond with enthusiasm to go OUTSIDE. Once outside, stay with us until you witness the desired results and praise us as we go. "Good, go potty outside!" Make us feel that we are the most special dog in the whole world. STAY with us until we go and make it abundantly clear what you want from us. Remember, we do not have these bathroom rules in our society, just in yours.

If you do not stay, you will miss the chance to praise, and you will miss the chance to name the behavior. "Outside" is where we need to go; "Go potty," "find a tree," or "do your business" (call it what you like) is what we need to do when we get there. If you stay with us, you'll also know that both duties were accomplished before we come back in. Many young puppies are distraught about being separated from their owners. They may spend the entire time while outside just sitting on the porch. It's unlikely that any pup or I will want to ask to go outside if it is a negative experience to be separated from the security of our human family.

Feed and exercise on a regular schedule. Remember, what goes in regularly will come out regularly. How soon after I eat do I need to go out? Keep track, usually within an hour. Free-choice feeding may hamper your house-training efforts—what trickles in will trickle out unpredictably! I know I probably need to go out immediately upon waking in the morning, soon after eating—about forty-five minutes—after napping, and after exercising. If you can anticipate when we need to go and hustle us to the appropriate spot at the first sign, you will avoid accidents.

Potty pads are one more step to get rid of if the ultimate goal is to get your pup to go outside, so if you must have an indoor toileting area in the interim, try a low-sided tray with a piece of sod or dirt to copy the surface of the intended outside target. In the very beginning, you may want to paper the entire area (if your pup stays in the laundry room, paper the entire area). That way there is no mistake. Use the method described above to teach your pup the exact spot you eventually want them to use. You begin to remove the papers over time so that only the final spot or tray is left with paper. You can also move the tray closer and closer to the outside door, until one day it is on the other side. In the long run, having an indoor potty area will slow down the process of getting the pup to go outside, so avoid it if you can.

If we have already soiled on the carpet or floor, it is imperative that you get a good enzyme cleaner to rid the area of any smell. Remember, we can smell what you cannot, and that odor triggers the elimination response. Make sure you are neutralizing odor on all the spots we use. Fresh spots will respond to white vinegar, but if a spot has dried before treatment, you need a bacterial enzyme-odor eliminator product such as Nature's Miracle. Either way, the product needs to soak deeply into the carpet pad. If your pet has an accident, swat yourself with the rolled up newspaper, not the dog. It was your fault for not watching closely enough! Rubbing our nose in it (yuck!), scolding, or hitting will only teach us to avoid you when we feel the need to eliminate, rather than come find you. Scolding us only teaches us to sneak off down the hall where you will not see us. It also tells us that you are not a good leader (you are stupid if you think we should never go potty). You can also increase separation anxiety, because it seems as if every time you leave the room, something happens out there, and you come back angry. Remember, we love you and want to do what is right; young pups just do not know what that is yet.

Summary

1. Never leave us unattended. If you cannot see us, we are eliminating in the wrong place. Use playpens, leash us to your belt, or use a kennel to help contain us. Remember, you only have to do this for a few weeks, until we learn your rules.
2. Kennels or crates should be large enough for us to stand up, turn around, and lie back down. If we can walk or step in the crate, we will eliminate in it. Never leave us in the crate more than the recommended time.
3. SCHEDULE. When I was young, I needed to be taken out for elimination first thing in the morning, then about forty-five minutes after scheduled meals, last thing at night, after napping, and after exercise. If your pup is very young, every hour or every other hour is a good time to try and eliminate.
4. Watch for elimination signals—we give them; some of us are more obvious than others.
5. When you take us to the elimination area, take us directly to our assigned toilet area and praise for quick results.
6. Stay with us to avoid separation anxiety, ensure we do all we are suppose to do, and praise us quickly for the correct results.
7. Be sure to name the activity so later we will eliminate on command.
8. If your carpet or floor has been soiled, it is imperative that you get a good enzyme cleaner to rid the area of any smell. We can smell even dead bacteria and that really triggers us to go again. Nature's Miracle or a similar enzyme cleaner is the most effective.

It will also help if we can let you know when we need to go outside. Hanging some Christmas bells on some ribbon down the door handle or a placing a bellhop type bell by the door is a great way for us to communicate with you. Every time you take us out to go potty, you hit the bell. We soon learn to hit that bell when we need to go out. It's easy and very effective.

Crate Training

Many dog owners think the use of a crate is a punishment. They forget wolves live in and love their dens. Crate training is a gift you give us. If crates are introduced properly, not only will we love them, but also they will help us be the perfect pet. They will assist us from elimination accidents, improper chewing habits, staying off the furniture habits, excessive barking and territory protection problems, and generally make for an exceeding well-balanced dog. So learn to love your crate! I remember how when I first saw that thing, I was not sure what it was. When I was playing on the floor in the living room, in the kitchen, in the bedroom, or any place, that *thing* was always there. Somehow, that crate kept moving to stay near me. Soon, I was accustomed to seeing that thing. Before long, the crate was filled with happy memories. Treats and toys were tossed in, and I chased them into the crate, or occasionally, I was petted as I wandered into this den. A few times, I found a biscuit tied to the back bar, and I sat in my den (crate) and ate my entire treat. The process:

> Door was always open at first. My human started to call this thing my den. When I first arrived to Bev's house, I would fall asleep on a towel on her lap. Later I found that towel in my den, and I had those pleasant memories and smells on that towel. I learned to love my den. Many months after, I learned the bathroom rules, so we did not have to use a crate; the cage door was always open. I still wanted to use my den. It was a safe, wonderful place for me to sleep or rest.

The Process

1. Select the correct size crate. We must be able to stand up, turn around, and lie down again; if we can walk in it, we can eliminate in it. If you have a large breed dog, like me, we will outgrow several expensive crates. So to save money, buy a large one that you fill and make smaller. (You can be creative with cardboard, pillows, etc.)
2. Make it smell like you. Put down a soft bed and cover it with your pillow case, a towel, or your T-shirt—something that has your smell, not laundry smell. We will feel much safer if your smell is all over this new fangled thing. Be sure all the bedding is washable. After the initial

introduction and several weeks of using the crate, you will want to wash the bedding for us.

3. Keep the crate open and near you and us pups at all times. The next phase begins with getting us into the crate with a treat or favorite toy and *gently* closing the door, then opening it again quickly. This should be repeated many times, leaving the door closed longer and longer. Then keep the door closed until we finish our favorite treat, our nap, etc.

4. The next phase begins by calling us into the crate, putting in a treat, closing the crate, and staying nearby—within sight—then coming over to the crate when we have settled down and open the crate. This should be done when we have just finished an extensive workout and are ready for a nap. Do this often. NEVER LET US OUT WHILE WE ARE WHINING OR DEMANDING. If you do, we have just taught you to come when called, and that noisemaking gets us out of the crate.

5. The next phase has you putting us into the crate for a much-longer period, while you are right next to us, watching TV, reading, etc. This begins with ten minutes and works up to an hour. Next, you leave the room for short periods of time and then extending the time you are out of the room little by little. Soon, we get very used to your absence while we spend time in our little den—the crate.

6. During this entire time, you can put us in the crate all night to sleep. We need to be next to your bed in the beginning so you can hear us whine (we will whine for both comfort and distress because we need to eliminate, do not open the door unless we need to eliminate). Remember, very young pups may need to eliminate every few hours in the beginning, eventually sleeping through the night. (Particularly if you pick up our water bowel early in the evening and exercise us so we eliminate just before we go down for the night.)

7. Continue to keep the crate open near us all the time; you will find we often prefer to go into the crate to rest. If you have small children, the crate should be off-limits to the humans, and we should feel very comfortable in our safe den.

8. Never use the crate as a punishment or time-out. Use a laundry room or bathroom for that. The crate must always be a positive thing for us.

9. Soon you will be able to put us into our crate for the recommended times (except for overnight sleeping):

a.   8-10-week-old puppies: 1 hour at a time in crate max

b.   11-12-week-old puppies: 2 hours at a time in crate max

c.   13-16-week-old puppies: 3 hours at a time in crate max

d.   17-20-plus-week-old puppies: 3.5 hours at a time in crate max. Don't do this on a regular basis; it is not good for our muscle tone and mental stimulation.

10. Eventually, we may not need our crate, but still want to use it occasionally as a den.

Sit

We are simple creatures. This is a very easy command for us to learn. After all, we do a lot of sitting during the day. This is how we become polite. We use sitting almost instead of saying please. Therefore, it is a very important command.

The "sit" position, sometimes in the beginning the hand needs to be closer to the muzzle

If you hold a treat very, very close to our nose—almost like you magnetized the treat and our nose—and you slowly bring it up above our head, we will often just sit. Sometimes we will back up to keep that treat in our view. If that happens, just start this exercise near a wall so we back up to the wall and then sit! Do not say the word "sit" yet; we do not know what it means. Wait until our bottom just hits the ground, and then say the word. If you do that enough times, we get that the action of sitting our bottoms on the ground means "sit." If we are having difficulty learning this command, if you just wait, and we know you have a treat, we will eventually sit, then you can say the word and give us our reward.

After about fifteen times, we should know the word "sit," and you should not have to have a treat in your hand to lure us into position. Always praise us, but the rewards can stop after about two dozen times. After we know this command by voice, you can start to add the hand command. Do the hand command, then the voice command. The gesture should look like a hand sweep up.

Down

This is a little harder for small dogs to learn. We larger dogs get this command easily. If we sit first, then you bring that treat close to our nose again—as if it was magnetized—and slowly bring it down, straight from our nose to the floor. We will follow that treat down, then slide the treat along the floor a little away from our heads, and we will continue to follow it into a down position. Therefore, you and the treat have sort of made an L shape. If you keep that treat close to my nose, close to my body, I find it easier to go into a down. Some dogs need a slightly different approach. Their bottoms keep popping up, especially the small breed dogs.

So here are some tricks. Sit on the floor and, with your leg extended out with a slight bend, make a little tunnel. Lure the little one over to you and hold the treat under your leg. Then keep luring your little fellow to follow the treat under your leg, and make that leg low enough that we need to lie down to get under that tunnel. After we lie down, say the word "down."

Some dogs need even more tricks to get this command. Another trick can be done near some stairs. Have your little one sit on one stair. Bring the treat from the nose, down, beyond the stair, down to the next step. Sometimes our nose will follow that treat all the way down, and we will end up in almost a down position. One last trick: when we get to that almost down position, say "down." Alternatively, just before we lie down, you can say the word "down," and we eventually get what that command means. Be flexible and ready to try a few things.

The "tunnel" approach to the DOWN command.

The hand gesture is generally a finger pointed down, in a downward sweep of the hand. Because Bev and I are often at the beach and I am far away and might not see a pointed hand command, she taught me that when she holds her hand way up in the air, it means I lie down.

Remember to practice sit and down separately, or we can easily get confused that "sit" and "down" mean the same thing.

Stay

This is one of the commands you humans goof up the most. You say that word all the time, and we often have no idea what you mean. Sometimes you say words that almost sound like "stay" like "hey," "ray," "way," so we get VERY confused. Help us really understand you. Leave no room for error and make us 100 percent successful. This is a process that will start at three seconds and should go up to twenty minutes. We will eventually extend the distance from one-eighth of an inch to one hundred yards or more, but it takes time!

Start the process by asking us to sit, while holding your hand up—like a halt sign—secure a treat with your thumb so we cannot steal it, and hold it up, right in front of our nose. We are so focused on this treat, we do not move.

We might try to steal it, but our bottoms usually stay on the floor. Hold this for only three seconds as you say "stay". Then say "release" or "free" and feed us the goodie. We just had a successful three-second stay. Do this for several days, several times a day. Then go to the next phase.

Next phase means holding the treat for a longer time, maybe five seconds, then up to ten seconds. Take time to proceed for longer times.

"Stay" when the hand is beginning to move away from our face

Next, you will move your hand for a brief moment away from our face. So as you hold the treat in a halt-type hand gesture, you say "stay" as you stand on our side and move your hand directly out from our face—then move it right back in front of our nose again. This gets us used to some distance away from the treat and your hand, but you are still right next to us so staying is easier. Over time, you will increase the time your hand is away from our face.

Next phase: You will stand directly in front of us, with your hand in a stay position—with a treat—and as you say "stay," you take a quick step away from us, and then quickly return, before we have a chance to get up and move. Over time, you will increase both the time and distance you move away from us.

ALWAYS walk back to right in front of us, so we do not move. After we learn "come" or the recall command, be sure to practice both commands separately. This is important because we do not want to think every stay is followed by a recall or movement. Sometimes we need to stay and not move—period.

Recall

This is another command you humans really goof up. You say "come" so many times, and we end up ignoring you at least half the time. This means we actually do not know what it means: return, go chase a ball, stay where we are, or ignore you. We really are not sure what that means. So let us start the process.

First, some rules. One hundred percent of the time, we must return to you and sit. Just coming toward you is not enough because we can easily get distracted and take off again, so a formal recall means come to you and sit. How do you get us 100 percent of the time to come? Never say the word without a leash attached. Use another word when the leash is not attached for now. Next, never use that word and follow it with anything but praise, happy voice, and delight. If you call me over and put a leash on me to go out of the wonderful dog park, I am not inclined to want to come to you again. If you yell at me or put me into the bath after I come to you, why should I come to you. Always make us feel when we come to you that we just won a trip to Disneyland. If you have to do something I find distasteful, make me sit, shake hands or stay until you separate the "come" command with at least 3 seconds of something else. That way I don't associate the recall with anything but joy.

Start in the living room, where there is nothing else to distract us, put a leash on us; and when we are wondering around, not looking at you, pick up the leash and say "come." Say it in the wonderful voice that really gets us. If we do not come, gently pull the leash so we end up in front of you. Using your hand command, lure us into a sit position. Now we are sitting in front of you after the "come" command. Repeat that several times. Sometimes you can be around a corner with a longer leash and try it there. SOMETIMES, not every time, you can put us into a stay and walk a short distance away and say "come."

Outside on walks, when we walk on ahead of you, you can suddenly say our name and command "come' as you walk backward, and we run to catch up to you and sit. So now, we are coming to you 100 percent of the time outside. Now we are ready for the next phase, which may be weeks later.

The next phase is where we add distractions and distance. Put a long rope or fifty-foot leash on us. Now you can practice "stay" and "come" at longer and longer distances—first in the house, then outside. We can go to the park and practice. When we are successful one hundred times out of one hundred, we can go to the next step. The next step is to take us to the park with our long fifty-foot leash on, and drop the leash and let us play. As we are playing and goofing around, go over and step on the leash as you yell "come." If we do not come, bend down, pick up the leash, and gently pull us in. DO NOT repeat the word, but make noises and whistles to encourage our approach and praise us as we come to you, just don't treat us until we sit in front of you. Try not to start this exercise when we are chasing a squirrel or in the middle of a play fight with our friends. Call us when there is a good chance we will come. I must tell you, when I'm chasing a squirrel, I literally cannot hear Bev calling me; I am zoned out. So practice when we have a good chance of hearing you and obeying.

After months of work, we may be ready for off-leash recall. If we fail, put us back on the leash so we do not think the meaning of that word has changed. Keep the leash on for several days again.

Loose Leash Walking/Heel

There is absolutely nothing in my world that prepares me for the heel command or walking without pulling on a leash. No dog would naturally walk to the left of a human or not run as fast as we wanted even with a leash attached. Our bodies are meant for pulling, so not pulling on a leash makes no sense. Therefore, this command must start out at home, inside where I can concentrate more. Outside there are too many distractions to get this crazy command.

Leave the leash on me, as we are just sitting around watching TV; eventually, I would get up to sniff something and the leash would get taunt, and Bev would say "close." When I heard that word, I would step back or move my head to see what she was talking about; the leash would get loose, and she threw me a treat. Soon, when I felt the collar get a bit tight against my neck, I knew that was not what she wanted. When she said that word, and my collar became comfortable again, I got a treat and that was what she wanted. I soon learned "close" meant no discomfort around my neck and a treat.

After about a week, we followed this exercise with going outside for a walk. When I pulled on my leash and my collar got tight, I heard a funny noise Bev makes that gets my attention, as she said the word "close," and when I moved back, slowed down, or made my collar loose again, she praised me.

Many dogs are not as brilliant as I am and will need more work. If they do not produce a loose leash when their human says "close," humans may need to "crazy walk."

Let me explain this "crazy walk." You, the human, will take one of us pooches for a walk. You walk along, and as long as the leash is loose and we are walking nicely on your left side, you praise us. If we lag behind, you encourage us with a voice and a treat. If we pull, you give your loud noise that gets our attention, and then you turn around and walk in the opposite direction. Then we will hurry up to catch up with you. Again, you praise us the entire time the leash is loose. If we pull, you make a noise and turn around again. Most of us prefer to walk in the same direction, so we will soon get the idea of walking in one direction, keeping our collars comfortable and not pull.

Some humans try the "tree" approach. The minute we pull on the leash, you stand very still until we stop pulling, then you keep walking. This can work on those of us that like to keep moving, but some of us canines love to be outside so much, we do not care if we stand in the same place for hours. So these are a few of the tricks for you humans to help us understand about not pulling. Finally, when I actually walk nicely near you, you can slip me a treat from your left hand near your left leg. I soon want to hang out there because I know that sometimes a treat will appear there.

Heeling

The next step is to teach us "heel." Again, this concept is very weird for me. It makes no wolf/dog sense. It is best to start inside again to reduce the distractions. I need to learn that "heel" means movement but close to your left side. So a game I like to play is the heel-sit-heel game. My human holds my leash loosely in her right hand; I am on her left side, she holds a treat in her left hand and holds it very close to my nose. She starts to walk with her left leg as she says "heel." I move to follow that treat, then after only one-step, she says, "sit." She repeats this about three times before she actually gives me that treat. She looks somewhat funny in this exercise, sort of like a military person on a weird march. Heel, sit, heel, sit—left foot forward, right foot even with the left, left foot forward, right foot comes up to the left.

After about a week of this one-step, we can actually try three or four steps without a sit to get that feel of walking close to my human. After another week of indoor practice, we can practice for short periods outside. Soon we can "heel" outside for short walks. After a few weeks, I will follow a hand without a treat, and after that, I am in the habit of heeling. Start slowly and keep practicing; remember this is a weird concept for me and most other dogs to understand.

Leave It

This may seem like a game to you, but for us, this command can save our lives. Do you know about radiator fluid? Even though it smells delicious to me, and tastes like candy, it is deadly poisonous. About two tablespoons for a dog my size (sixty-five pounds) will kill me. One tablespoon will ruin my kidneys for life. For a small guy, a dog about ten pounds, a few licks will kill him. So when we are walking, we are thirsty, and we come upon a puddle and begin to drink it; a "leave it" may just save my life if I listened. You may find it useful when you drop candy, meat, pills, or anything on the floor, and to prevent me from gobbling it up, a "leave it" could be fantastic. So let us begin.

Start by holding a treat in your hand so that I cannot get it (this is very important or I may think the game is "steal it"). Hold your hand very close to my face and say "leave it." At first, we will try to get that treat for several minutes. You need to calmly repeat "leave it" many times. Don't move your hand. There will be a moment, a very brief moment, when we will stop trying to get that treat. We might look away for a second. It is that second that you must command "take it," open your hand, and let me have that treat. Repeat this fun game five or six times in a row, several times a day. This is a game I love to play and really learn "leave it." Be careful not to hold the treat too far away from me, it needs to by very close.

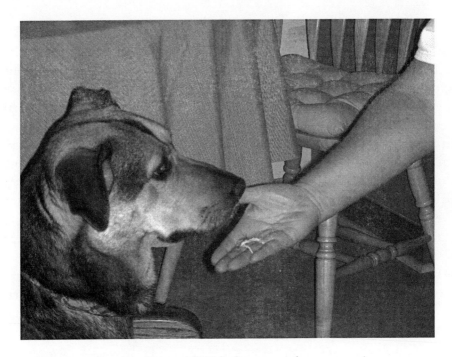

"Leave it" with the open palm

Next phase begins when ten out of ten times I do not even attempt to go for the treat until you say "take it." Then you do the same game with an open palm. The treat is in the open palm that you can close and prevent me from taking the treat if I forgot what "leave it" means. When I leave the open palm treat every time for at least ten times; we go to the next step.

The next step is putting the treat on the floor, just under my nose as I sit over it, and your hand is nearby to prevent any mistakes I may make. When I can leave the treat until the "take it," then we go to the next step. The next step is for the human to walk away from the treat and release me or let me take it when you are several feet away. When I master this phase, you can drop something as you say "leave it" and keep practicing this great game.

Along with the first stage of learning this game, you can play an outside version of the game. As we are walking and I go over to smell a bush or other object of interest, you say "leave it," gently pull me away, and then treat me. Soon I really understand what "leave it" means and helps me be a good citizen.

This is a command that can be used to leave unhealthy food or forbidden objects alone, and for leaving people or other dogs alone. This is such a useful communication tool.

Drop It

This is actually a very different command than "leave it." "Leave it" means I never have the object in my mouth. "Drop it" means I have something in my mouth, and I need to open my jaws to drop it. This should be the ultimate trade game. Let me explain.

Let us play tug-of-war. We are having a great time; I have the tug toy firmly in my mouth when you say "drop it" as a tasty treat appears before my eyes. I drop the toy to take the treat. Then you give me the toy right back. WOW! "Drop it" means get a treat. Of course, I am going to learn that one fast. There is no downside. I drop the toy to get a treat, and I get the toy back. We play this for a few weeks, and soon I will not need a treat every time, just some praise. I really learned this one fast.

Stop Jumping

The need for me to get to your face is both learned and innate. Baby wolves would lick their mom's mouth to get some food; I love to lick Bev's face because I love her and am happy to see her, and I like to be as high as she is. Therefore, for many reasons, I jump up. This often works. When I jump on people, they pay attention to me. OK, some of that attention is shouting or yelling no or "off," or touching me as I was pushed away, but it got me ATTENTION! Sometimes people just pet me when I jump on them, so jumping has been successful. This is before I was taught better manners.

We started by not allowing me to touch humans when I jumped. Bev would shout her loud noise to get my attention as she jumped backward. Then she immediately told me to sit, then gave me lots of attention, her face, and a treat. Soon I learned that to get her face, instead of jumping, I would sit. We would play games where she would run up to me in an excited voice and say hi, and almost try to get me to jump. If I went to jump, she would remind me with her distraction noise, a jump back, and tell me to sit. We played this game over and over again in the quiet of our living room until I really got the habit of sitting instead of jumping to say hello.

She reinforced this whenever she came home—I really wanted to jump on her then. Instead, she would tell me to sit when she was on the other side of the door to my space. She would slowly open the door, and if I were not sitting, she would close the door again without coming in and say "sit." Sometimes she held a treat down low to help me remember to sit. Now I sit (OK, my tail is wagging so hard, my butt is brushing sideways on the floor, but it is sitting), until she is in the door, bends down to my face, and says "free." Then I lick her like crazy.

She helped me learn not to jump on others by always having a leash attached when we met people. When I jumped, she would shout her attention noise and tell me to "sit" as she gently tugged the leash so I could not touch the humans. Then when I was sitting, they would hug me. I loved this sit game.

Also, I am not allowed to greet people at our door at home. When the doorbell rings, I was taught to go to my mat downstairs, away from the door. Now, the temptation to jump with all the excitement at a door is taken away. Instead of jumping, I have the habit of sitting to greet people.

No Bite

When I was a young lad, I used my mouth to explore everything. Biting was just a way for me to test the world. When I bit other little puppies, they yelped and helped me learn bite inhibition (which is one reason puppy play is so critical). Humans need to do the same thing. The minute our mouth touches a human skin or clothes, we need to hear a high-pitched loud yelp. Then we need a soft suitable chew toy given to us with praise so we understand what you want. If we ignore you and continue to bite you, you need to yelp again and walk away. We hate isolation. We will learn quickly that you humans have tissue paper—thin skin, and we cannot mouth you. When you give us the feedback, like a fellow dog, we get what you want much faster. If you yell no or "no bite," we do not know what you want; we only know you are excited. Sometimes, we think that means to play harder. Yelping and substituting an appropriate toy or isolation works very quickly.

Well, those are the most important basic obedience commands that have worked very well for me. I have not discussed excessive barking, digging too much, destructive chewing or a few other misbehaviors but if you need more information, you can reach me at *www.pawsitivethinking.com* and just ask. Of course, I've learned many other commands or tricks, all with the same method; lure me into the position you want, reward, after a while name it, release and repeat. If done with a happy attitude and voice, a few minutes several times a day, it's a breeze! Hope my prospective has helped with the simple idea of obedience training. Remember, training will only be successful if you employ the S.C.A.L.E.

Final Howlings

Development Stages

I wanted to prepare you humans for some changes your puppies may go through. We have different stages that will affect our training. You do not need to know all of them, just the ones that may make the biggest impact on us. When we are very young, up to about six months old or so, we have a puppy license. This means we are usually more curious than fearful, we do not know the rules of dog communication, we do not know human culture (bathroom rules), we do not have our full set of regular teeth yet, we are learning bite inhibition, and the entire world is new and exciting. This is where socialization is very important. This is the stage in my life when if you are fearful and upset, I learn to be fearful. If you are happy and easy, I learn to be easy. This is the time when my habit formation is very important—learning to brush my teeth, preparing me for the groomers, clipping my nails, potty training, learning to say please (sit), and learning basic obedience.

After six months old, puppies lose their license; male hormones start to escalate sharply, female hormones begin to rise, and the fear imprinting stage can begin. This is where more fearful and more aggressive behavior can suddenly appear. This is why socialization is as critical now as when we were puppies. This is why introductions to bikes, vacuum cleaners, and the rest of the world are better if it is done earlier. Exposure should continue and any fearful behavior nipped in the bud, not by avoidance, but by getting us used to whatever is scaring us.

Because puppies have lost their puppy license, it means older dogs may need to teach them better manners. I will tolerate a puppy's obnoxious behavior until they begin to lose that license. When those young ones get to that age, suddenly I will growl or snap if my other communication was not heeded. It seems to upset most humans, so I better prepare you for this.

You will take the dog in your life out to play, and at about six months old, suddenly he will get into more quarrels and fights, particularly with older dogs. This is important for the pup's proper development; we are the only ones that can teach them proper dog manners. Now, if your pup is a male, his escalating hormones will upset me, and many other males, even though we are neutered. The hormones offend us. Therefore, your sweet little guy may be picked on. If you decide not to neuter your boy, just be prepared for more scuffles. If you decide not to neuter you girl, be prepared for some very rough male approaches if she is near her "time". Her hormonal swings make for some very moody behavior. After a few months of socializing with us big boys, little pups, both males and females learn proper communicating with other dogs.

At about one year old, you may think you have the perfect pet. AHA! We fool you because, at about eighteen months old, we enter our "teenage" years. We are obstinate, mischievous, and will test the limits. Do not be surprised; just keep your leadership exercises very strong during this time. Another refresher obedience class may also be of value. This stage may last until two or three human years.

Then you can relax—no more growth stages that will affect behavior until old age, when moodiness, hurt joints, and ministrokes can affect our actions. I share this information with you to help you and prepare you, so there are fewer surprises.

Obedience Training for Life

If you are practicing good leadership, it means I'm practicing my commands all the time. Progress can be achieved by taking any of the basic commands and add in more distance, more time and more distractions. For example, "stay" is practiced in the house (with few distractions) and you add in more time, so we can stay down for twenty minutes at a time. You also add in distance so I will stay down when you are twenty or forty feet away. Then you can add in more distractions. Now we can practice "stay" at a park with lots of people around, then practice at a dog park where there are many dogs around. One of the games we play in Bev's advanced class is we all line up in a row while the humans walk away to form another line about thirty feet away. Then one human at a time will call their dog's name and "come." Only that dog is allowed to move. If a dog makes a mistake and moves when their name is not called, their human comes running over to help them into a sit and stay.

Taking another obedience class each year helps to keep us pooches and you humans stay sharp and our communication very effective and fun.

Remember to use the S.C.A.L.E. If you want us canines to be happy and listen to you, we must have our needs met. I hope my howlings help you have a pawsitively fantastic time with your adorable four-legged housemate. Well, I think I'm barked out and need to go get some sun and snooze a bit. Good luck and take care.

Authors that Helped Bev Understand Me (Dozer)[1]

Dr. Ian Dunbar
VCR: *Dog Aggression—Biting*
Dog Aggression—Fighting
Training the Companion Dog 1, *2*, *3*, and *4*

Dr. Dunbar's Good Little Dog Book
Before & After Getting your Puppy: The Positive Approach
How to Teach a New Dog Old Tricks
Dog Behavior: An Owner's Guide to a Happy Healthy Pet

Jean Donaldson
Culture Clash
Dogs Are from Neptune

Patricia McConnell
How to Be the Leader of the Pack
The Cautious Canine
Feeling Outnumbered? with Karen London
Feisty Fido with Karen London
The Other End of the Leash

Karen Pryer
Don't Shoot the Dog
Clicker Training for Dogs

Pamela Reid
Excel-erated Learning

---

[1] Some of these books gave Bev great understanding; some contributed very little, but they all helped.

Turid Rugaas
DVD: *Calming Signals*

On Talking Terms with Dogs
My Dog Pulls. What do I do?

Brenda Aloff
Aggression in Dogs
Canine Body Language

Emma Parson
Click to Calm

D. Caroline Colie
Beyond Fetch

Temple Grandin and Catherine Johnson
Animals in Translation: Using the Mysteries of Autism to Decode Animal Behavior

Stanley Coren
How to Speak Dog: Mastering the Art of Dog-Human Communication

Jana Murphy
The Secret Lives of Dogs: The Real Reasons Behind 52 Mysterious Canine Behaviors

Bruce Fogle and Anne B. Wilson
The Dog's Mind: Understanding Your Dog's Behavior

Roger Abrantes, Alice Rasmussen, and Sarah Whitehead
Dog Language: An Encyclopedia of Canine Behavior

Monks of New Skete
How to Be your Dog's Best Friend

Ceasar Milan
Cesar's Way: The Natural, Everyday Guide to Understanding and Correcting Common Dog Problems